Kids Cook: Global Recipes

for Meals, Sweets and Snacks

Tamia Sheldon

Quiz Included

To A. as always and to all the awesome young chefs who's hard work and delicious recipes created this cookbook.

eISBN: 978-1-5324-1345-2
Paperback ISBN: 978-1-5324-1346-9

Published in the United States by Xist Publishing
www.xistpublishing.com
PO Box 61593 Irvine, CA 92602

Download a free eBook copy of this book using this QR code.*

or at http://xist.pub/d8283

* Limited time only
Your name and a valid email address are required to download.
Must be redeemed by persons over 13

xist Publishing

Quiz

What recipe should you make?
Take this quiz and see.
Check off the color that is the best fit and see what recipe is a match.

- Nachos
- Galette
- Papaya Salad
- Kale Chips
- Banana Cupcakes
- Fried Rice
- Katsu Burger

Spicy

Sweet

Sour

Crunchy

Chewy

Hot

Cold

Salty

Savory

Morning

Noon

Night

Super hungry

After school snack

Have lots of time

Limited time

Blueberry Galette

Vegan

 50-60

Blueberry Galette

Ingredients

Dough:

1.5 cups flour
2 tsp. granulated sugar
1/2 tsp. table salt
11 Tbs.cold, vegan butter
3-5Tbs. very cold water

Filling:

4 cups blueberries
1/4 cup granulated sugar
2 Tbs. Vanilla
1 tsp. finely grated lemon zest
1 Tbs. all-purpose flour
2 tsp.table salt

◯ Preheat over to 350° F

1. Combine the flour, sugar, and salt

2. Cut the butter into cubes and add them to the flour. Smoosh together with clean hands.

3. Add ice water and still until dough comes together. Place in fridge while prepping fruit.

4. Place blueberries, sugar, salt, lemon zest, vanilla and flour into a big bowl, stir carefully.

5. On a floured surface, roll the dough into a round that's about 13 to 14 inches in diameter.

6. Spoon filling on top of dough, than fold all sides over to create a edge.

◯ Bake the tart until the pleats of dough are completely golden brown 25-30 minutes.

7. Let cool for at least 30 min to allow fruit to set up.

♥ Enjoy with ice cream or whipped coconut cream!

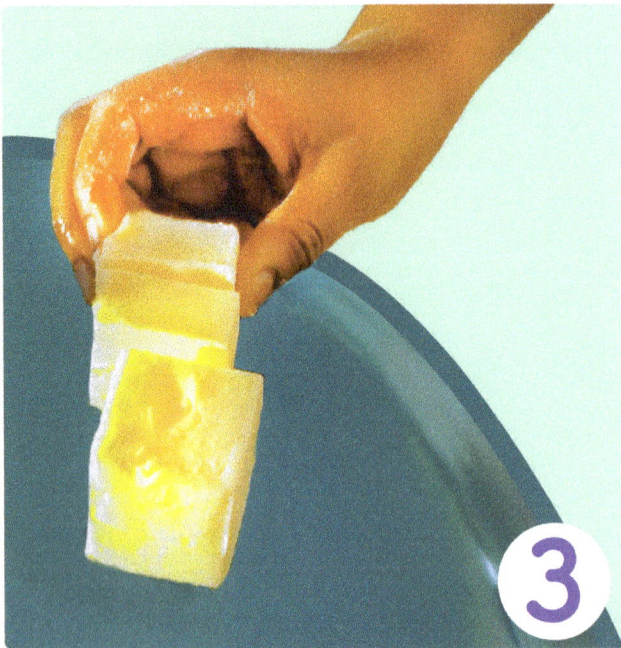

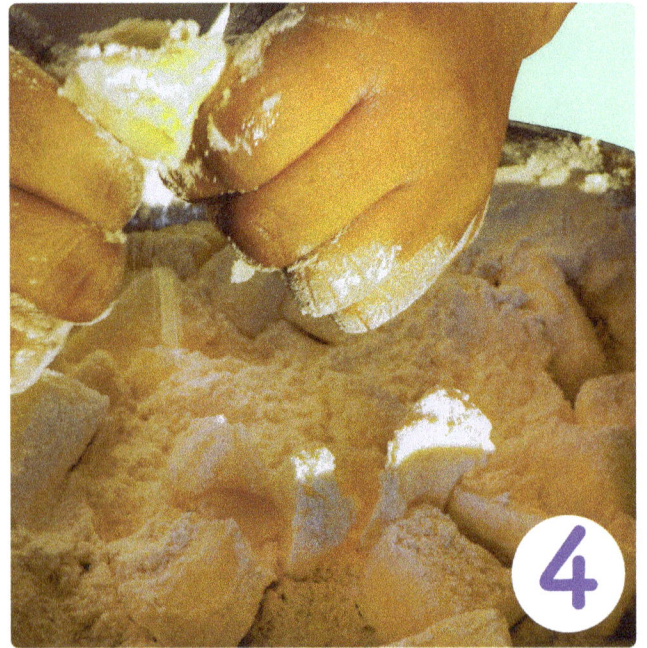

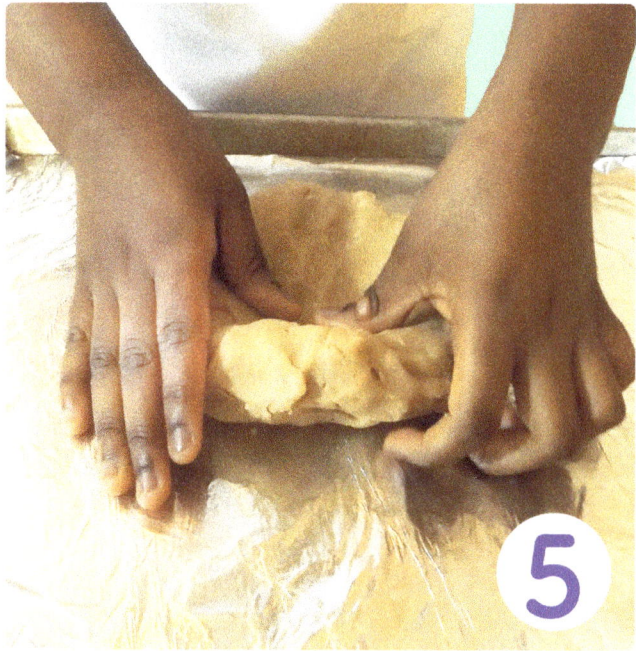

5

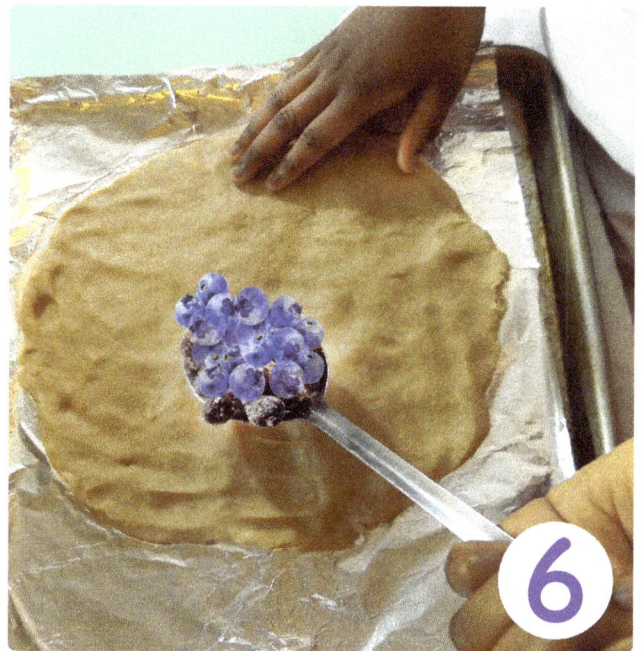

6

7

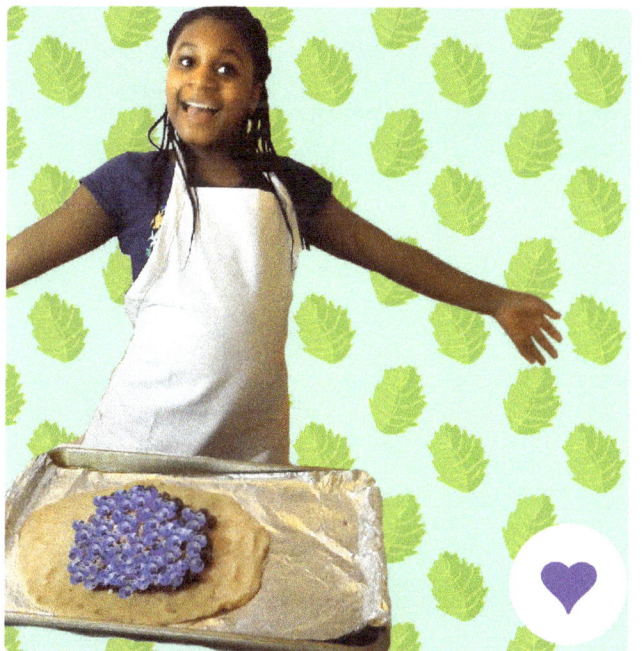

♥

Banana Cupcakes

Vegan

30-45

St. Lucian Banana Cupcakes

Dry Ingredients:

- 3/4 cups sugar
- 2 tsp. cinnamon
- 2 cups all-purpose flour
- 1 tsp. baking soda
- 1/2 tsp. baking powder
- 1/2 tsp. salt

Wet Ingredients:

- 2 1/2 cups mashed bananas
- 3/4 cups vegetable oil
- 2 tsp. vanilla

Frosting:

1 cup powdered sugar
1/2 teaspoon vanilla
1-2 tablespoons coconut milk

Mix to create frosting!

○ **Preheat oven to 350.**

❶ Slice Bananas.

❷ Add oil, vanilla, and bananas in a large bowl and mix well.

❸ Add Sugar.

❹ Add Flour.

❺ Add Salt and Cinnamon.

❻ Stir dry and wet ingredients together until very well mixed.

❼ Spoon muffin batter into a muffin tin.
(Use paper cups or grease the pan well with oil.)

○ **Bake with an adults help for 18-20 min.**

♡ Let muffins cool for 30 minutes and frost if desired.

1

2

3

4

5

6

7

Katsu Burger

Vegetarian Katsu Burger

Ingredients:

- 2 Tbsp rice milk
- Panko (Japanese breadcrumbs)
- Nutmeg
- Ketchup
- Tonkatsu sauce
- Small onion
- Vegetable Oil
- Salt & Pepper
- Meat substitute (Lightlife gimme lean sausage)
- 1 large egg

1. Dice Onion, add oil and onion to pan and fry until done
2. Pour panko into large mixing tray
3. Measure out salt and nutmeg and add to mix
4. Pour milk over panko and add "meat" and onions
5. Crack egg into mixing tray and mix very well with hands
6. Wet hands and form into balls and flatten into patties
7. Wash hands with warm water
8. Pour katsu sauce, ketchup into bowl
9. Stir well
10. Put burgers into pan, fry lightly on both sides
11. Pour sauce into pan, cook over low heat for 10 min

1

2

3

4

5

6

7

8

9

10

11

♥

Green Papaya Salad

Dairy Free

 **30-45**

Green Papaya Salad

Ingredients:

- 5 tablespoons fresh lime juice
- 3 tablespoons (packed) palm sugar or golden brown sugar
- 2 tablespoons plus 2 teaspoons fish sauce
- 3 Chinese long beans, halved crosswise or 15 green beans
- 1 1 1/2- to 13/4-pound green papaya, peeled, halved, seeded
- 10 large cherry tomatoes, halved

1. Have an adult help grate green papaya with a vegetable grater.
2. Place papaya in large bowl.
3. Squeeze lime until all the juice is out.
4. Add the palm sugar to lime juice and stir.
5. Add the fish sauce to lime juice and stir.
6. Slice green beans and add to bowl.
7. Slice tomatoes and add to bowl.
- Stir all ingredients, use a mortar if you have one to pound all ingredients together.

1

2

3

4

5

6

7

♥

V E G T A B L E

Fried Rice

Dairy Free

 30-45

Vegtable Fried Rice

Ingredients:

- 2 Tbsp. oil (canola or vegetable oil)
- 1 small onion (or ½ large onion), diced
- 1/2 c. frozen peas and carrots (or frozen peas)
- 2 cups cooked rice (*see note below)
- 1 tsp. sesame oil
- 2 eggs
- 2 scallions, chopped
- ¼ tsp. salt, plus more to taste
- Pinch of black pepper, plus more to taste

1. Dice onion and scallion.
2. Have an adult help heat the oil in a large saute pan over medium heat.
3. Add the diced onion and frozen peas, stirring occasionally with a spatula until the onion becomes soft and translucent.
4. Break up any big chunks of rice, add to pan and stir until rice has softened.
5. Drizzle the sesame oil over the rice mixture, and sprinkle in the salt and pepper.
6. Move the rice from the middle of the pan to make a hole in the middle of the rice and crack the two eggs into the hole.
7. As the eggs begin to cook, use the spatula to scramble and break up the eggs.
8. Sprinkle scallions over rice, salt and peppter to taste and serve hot.

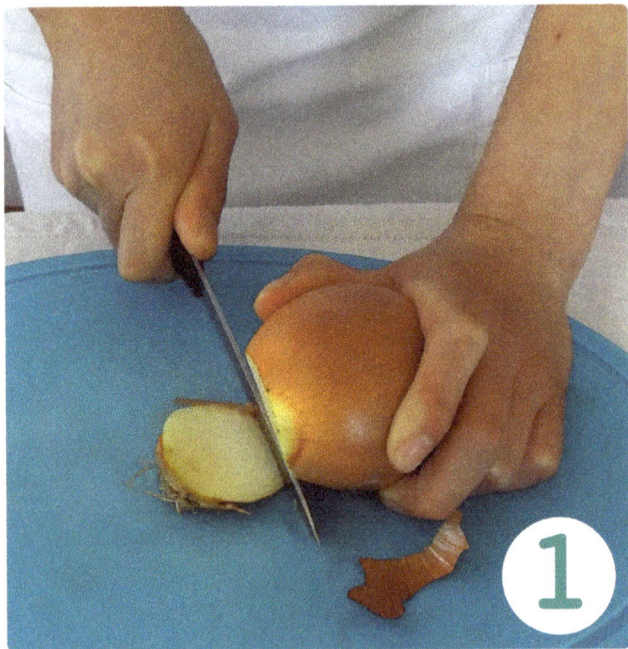

1

2

3

4

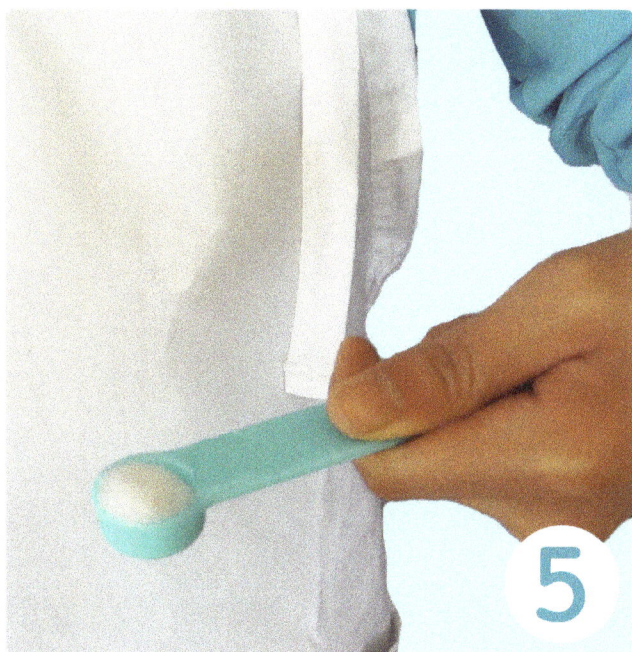

5

6

7

♥

Nachos

Vegatarian

20-25

Nachos!

Ingredients:
- 2 Tbsp. oil (canola or vegetable oil)
- 1 small onion (or ½ large onion), diced
- 1 small tomato diced
- Small bunch of green onions
- 8-12 oz chedder cheese
- Black olives
- Corn chips
- Sour Cream
- Salsa

1. Dice onion.
2. Dice tomato
3. Dice scallion.
4. Drizzle or spray oil over baking tray.
5. Layer chips, cheese, vegtables, cheese.
6. Bake with adults help for 12-15 min.
7. Have adult remove from oven and add sour cream & salsa.
♥ Enjoy!

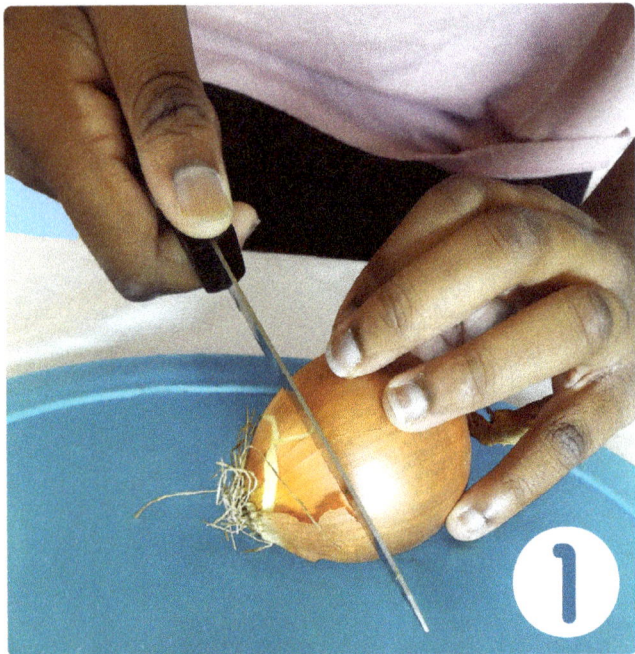

1

2

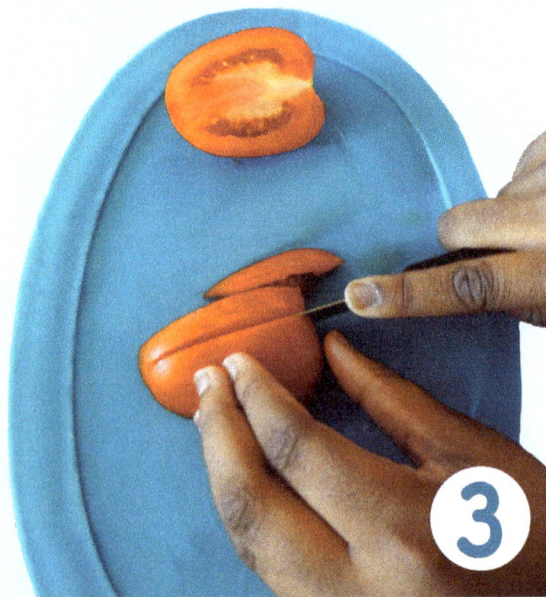

3

4

5

6

7

Kale Chips

Vegan

15-20

Roasted Kale Chips

Ingredients: Organic Kale, Olive Oil, Sea Salt.

Before you start wash and dry kale.
The drier the leaves, the crisper your chips !

○ Preheat oven to 350.

1 Tear Kale into small, bite size pieces.

2 Measure out 8 -10 cups of Kale into a large bowl.

3 Add 1/4 cup Olive Oil, lightly coat each leaf.

4 Add Salt, start with a 1/2 teaspoon. Less is more!

5 Vigorously squeeze ingredients together!

6 Place on baking pan, keep kale well spaced on pan.

○ Bake with an adults help for 10-12 min,
keep a VERY close eye on kale.

7 Cool for 2-5 min on a glass plate.

♥ Enjoy!

1

2

3

4

5

6

7

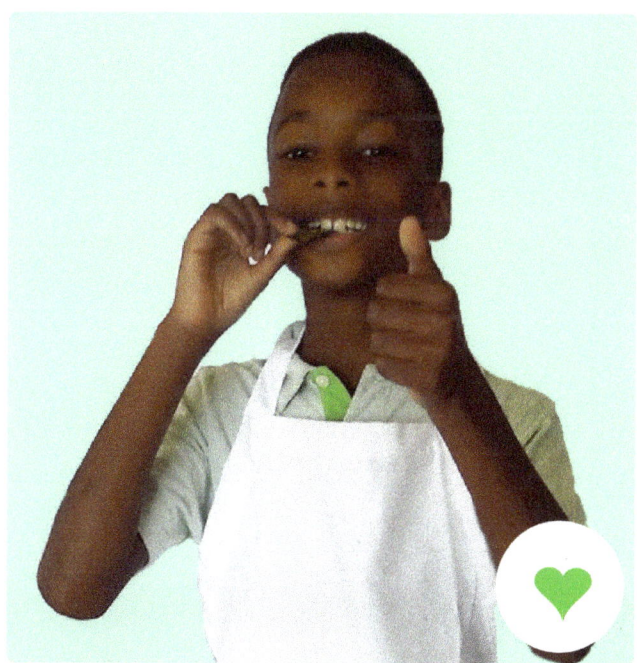

♥

CPSIA information can be obtained
at www.ICGtesting.com
Printed in the USA
LVHW070526030820
662227LV00017B/387

9 781532 413469